Birds are beautiful, graceful, majestic, and wonderful creatures. But sometimes they can be... **Bad Birds.**

For Jane and Neil

© Jack Wilcox, 2020

All rights reserved. This book or any portion there of may not be reproduced or used in any manner without permission from the author... But seriously, I'd probably never find out either way. So it's basically like an honor system or like returning the shopping cart.

Bad Birds
of North America

by Jack Wilcox

The Blue Jay is sometimes
mean to other birds
and can be very loud...

Can we turn the
volume down, Blue Jay?

The Red-winged Blackbird
can be a bully and hog
all the food at bird feeders...

Are we being a good sharer,
Red-winged Blackbird?

Canada Geese gather
in large flocks, and they
poop all over the place...

Canada Goose, that's gross!

The Northern Mockingbird
tends to nest in towns,
but it will go after anyone
who gets too close to its nest...

Calm down,
Northern Mockingbird.

The Bald Eagle sometimes swoops in to steal food that another bird is eating...

Bald Eagle,
that doesn't belong to you!

The Great Black-backed Gull
is the largest gull in the world,
and it can be very bold.
It takes food from other birds
and even people...

Great Black-backed Gull,
are we being nice to our friends?

A Northern Flicker once pecked a bunch of holes in the external fuel tank of a rocket ship. The launch was delayed and it caused lots of damage…

Northern Flicker, we do not peck holes in external fuel tanks!

The House Sparrow kicks other birds out of their bird house...

Naughty House Sparrow!

The Common Grackle
eats other birds' eggs...

Don't eat that egg,
Common Grackle!

The Brown-headed Cowbird
lays its eggs in other birds' nests
so the other birds end up feeding
and caring for its young...

Aw come on, Brown-headed Cowbird!

The American Wigeon,
a dabbling duck, finds its food
close to the water's surface.
Sometimes it steals food from
diving ducks that dive
deep down to find it...

American Wigeon,
is that the right thing to do?

The House Wren has been known to poke holes in other birds' eggs...

House Wren, go apologize right now!

The European Starling gathers in flocks in the tens of thousands and eats the most nutritious parts of cattle feed...

That's not your food, European Starling!

Oh! Here is the beautiful Yellow Warbler. It migrates thousands of miles every year and sings a sweet sounding song.

The daddy Yellow Warbler even helps the mommy Yellow Warbler build their nest...

Very good, Yellow Warbler!

Uh! That Yellow Warbler just took a stick out of another Yellow Warbler nest...

Bad Yellow Warbler!
All of the birds are being bad!

OTHER BIRDS
featured in this book

WHITE-THROATED SPARROW

LAUGHING GULL

CACKLING GOOSE
(smaller than Canada Goose with shorter beak and neck)

CAROLINA CHICKADEE

SONG SPARROW

EASTERN BLUEBIRD

CANVASBACK

OSPREY

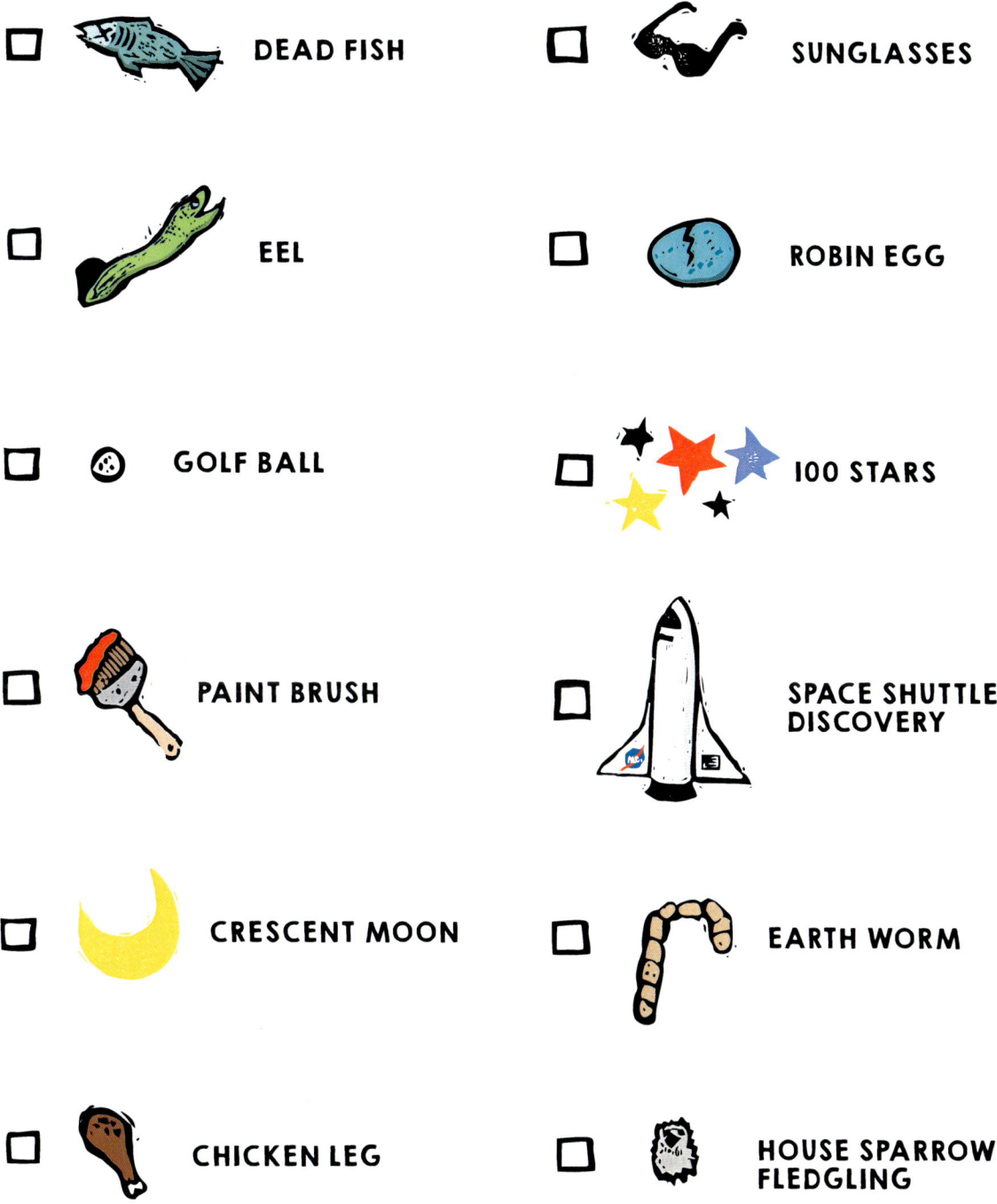

Made in United States
North Haven, CT
22 June 2023